THE ANIMAL FILES
WE NEED
PRAIRIE DOGS

by June Smalls

D1709496

WWW.FOCUSREADERS.COM

Focus Readers is distributed by North Star Editions:
sales@northstareditions.com | 888-417-0195

Produced for Focus Readers by Red Line Editorial.

Content Consultant: Laurel Hartley, Associate Professor of Integrative Biology, University of Colorado Denver

Photographs ©: Patrick_Gijsbers/iStockphoto, cover, 1; Warren Price Photography/Shutterstock Images, 4–5; David Butler/iStockphoto, 6; Laurie O'Keefe/Science Source, 9; KenCanning/iStockphoto, 10–11; Red Line Editorial, 12; Kerry Hargrove/Shutterstock Images, 15; miroslav_1/iStockphoto, 16–17; StefaniePayne/iStockphoto, 18–19; AHPhotoswpg/iStockphoto, 21; ESK Imagery/Shutterstock Images, 22; Pat Caulfield/Science Source, 24–25; Rick Bowmer/AP Images, 27; Chet Brokaw/AP Images, 29

Library of Congress Cataloging-in-Publication Data
Names: Smalls, June, 1984- author.
Title: We need prairie dogs / by June Smalls.
Description: Lake Elmo, MN : Focus Readers, [2019] | Series: The animal files
    | Audience: Grade 4 to 6. | Includes index. |
Identifiers: LCCN 2018027804 (print) | LCCN 2018028115 (ebook) | ISBN
    9781641854870 (PDF) | ISBN 9781641854290 (e-book) | ISBN 9781641853132
    (hardcover : alk. paper) | ISBN 9781641853712 (paperback : alk. paper)
Subjects: LCSH: Prairie dogs--Ecology--Juvenile literature. | Prairie
    dogs--Conservation--Juvenile literature.
Classification: LCC QL737.R68 (ebook) | LCC QL737.R68 S57 2019 (print) | DDC
    599.36/7--dc23
LC record available at https://lccn.loc.gov/2018027804

Printed in the United States of America
Mankato, MN
October, 2018

ABOUT THE AUTHOR
June Smalls is a writer and animal lover. She lives in Virginia with her husband, daughter, and an array of odd pets. Since she's never been out West, she's only seen prairie dogs in zoos.

TABLE OF CONTENTS

CHAPTER 1

LIFE IN A COLONY

Under the hot sun, a **colony** of prairie dogs is hard at work. The animals dig tunnels, feed on grass, and look for **predators**. Soon, one of the prairie dogs spots a coyote. The prairie dog barks out a warning call. The other prairie dogs run and hide.

A prairie dog jumps and lets out a call. This action is called a jump-yip.

Grasslands National Park in Canada is home to colonies of black-tailed prairie dogs.

Once the coyote leaves, a prairie dog stands tall. It throws its arms out and its head back. Then it lets out a high-pitched call. Other prairie dogs join in. This is how they check in on one another.

Prairie dogs are not dogs at all. They got their name from their call, which sounds like a dog's bark. Prairie dogs are actually rodents. They are related to squirrels and chipmunks. Most prairie dogs are 12 to 15 inches (30 to 38 cm) long and weigh up to 3 pounds (1.4 kg).

Prairie dogs live in the grasslands of central and western North America. Here, the animals dig large underground colonies made up of tunnels, or burrows.

EXPERT DIGGERS

Prairie dogs have short, muscular legs and sharp claws. These features help the animals dig complex tunnels. In 1901, scientists found a huge prairie dog colony in Texas. It covered 25,000 square miles (64,750 sq km). As many as 400 million prairie dogs lived inside.

Prairie dog families, called coteries, share the burrows. A coterie usually has one male, a few females, and their pups. Pups are baby prairie dogs. The adults defend their burrows from the rest of the colony.

A burrow has rooms called chambers. Prairie dogs have chambers for sleeping, eating, raising pups, and going to the bathroom. They also have chambers near exits. These chambers are where the prairie dogs listen for predators.

Prairie dogs may be small, but they are a keystone species. This means they affect the local **ecosystem**. When prairie dog populations change, other animal populations are affected.

At least nine other species depend on prairie dogs for survival. Some of these species hunt prairie dogs. Others live in the prairie dogs' burrows. Without prairie dogs, these species could lose important sources of food and shelter.

A HOME ON THE PRAIRIE

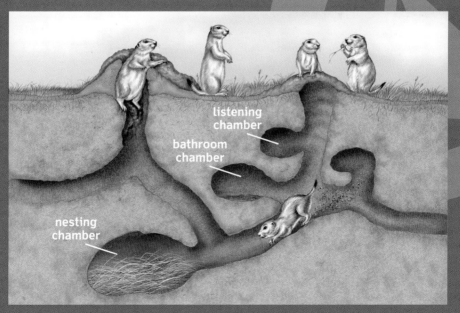

listening chamber

bathroom chamber

nesting chamber

CHAPTER 2

THE GRASSLANDS

Without prairie dogs, grasslands could lose much of their wildlife. Many plants and animals would be threatened. Some species, such as the black-footed ferret, could die out completely.

Five species of prairie dogs burrow across the North American grasslands.

The prairie dog helps create an ecosystem filled with many animals and plants.

These animals play an important role in grassland habitats. Their colonies can stretch for miles. Thousands of prairie dogs live in these burrows. Other animals

PRAIRIE DOG RANGES

Prairie dogs live in ranges throughout the United States, Mexico, and Canada.

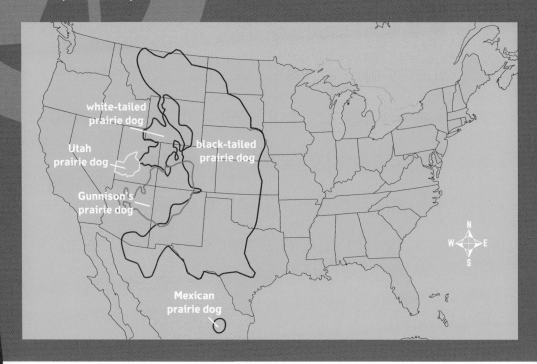

live there, too. Owls, snakes, ferrets, badgers, and even turtles will move into prairie dog burrows. Some of these animals are predators.

Prairie dogs keep careful watch for predators. They eat tall plants to make clearings. This helps them spot predators. They also make mounds on their tunnel entrances. By standing on top of the mounds, the prairie dogs can see farther. They call out to alert others of danger.

Despite these defenses, many animals eat prairie dogs. Coyotes, foxes, and bobcats are common predators. Prairie dogs are also the main source of food for the **endangered** black-footed ferret.

Since prairie dog populations have decreased, the black-footed ferret now has less to eat.

Prairie dogs eat grasses and other plants. The clippings from their meals, along with their waste, help **fertilize** the ground. Seeds grow better in the fertilized soil. Plants above prairie dog colonies have more **nutrients**. Cattle prefer eating these healthier plants.

Prairie dogs' eating habits cause more flowers to grow, too. Flowers attract insects such as bees and butterflies. These pollinators help even more plants grow. In this way, prairie dogs support the growth of the ecosystem.

A black-footed ferret looks out of a prairie dog burrow.

Prairie dogs also help control some plants, such as mesquite. This type of plant can be harmful to cattle. Prairie dogs eat the plants' seeds. They also strip bark from young seedlings. As a result, they prevent mesquite from growing. Areas with mesquite tend to suffer from **erosion**. By controlling mesquite, prairie dogs help keep soil from eroding.

PRAIRIE DOG TALK

Prairie dogs are social animals. To greet one another, prairie dogs kiss. They touch their noses and lock their teeth. This helps them identify one another. It may also tell them what the other has eaten.

Prairie dogs communicate mainly by making noises. They bark, snarl, growl, scream, and yip. They use different warning calls based on the type of predator they see. Prairie dogs also click their teeth. This sound can be heard up to 300 feet (91 m) away.

Other animals benefit from the sounds prairie dogs make. For instance, owls overhear prairie dog calls. When a prairie dog barks, the owl knows to look out for predators.

An adult prairie dog and pup greet each other.

CHAPTER 3

PROBLEMS FOR PRAIRIE DOGS

Humans use grasslands for farming, raising cattle, and building cities. The more grasslands humans use, the less land there is for prairie dogs. Over time, prairie dogs could lose their habitats.

Many farmers do not want prairie dogs on their farms. Prairie dogs graze on farmers' crops and feed on open fields.

Prairie dog burrows can get in the way of human activity.

Ranchers worry there won't be enough plants for their cattle. Prairie dogs' digging creates other problems. Farm equipment can get caught in the rodents' holes. These problems cost farmers money.

Some farmers try to remove prairie dogs from their farms. They poison or shoot the animals. Construction is another threat to prairie dogs. When humans bulldoze land, they kill the colonies that live there.

Small populations of prairie dogs live in cities. When it is time for these prairie dogs to mate, they can't easily move to other colonies. They have fewer partners

A landowner flags a prairie dog burrow for removal.

to choose from. Scientists worry that this will cause lower genetic diversity. Genetic diversity is the number of different traits present in a species. Species with greater genetic diversity are more likely to **adapt** to their environment. This gives them a greater chance of survival.

In 2009, plague spread to prairie dogs in Badlands National Park in South Dakota.

Prairie dog populations are also threatened by plague. This disease is deadly to prairie dogs. It spreads from rodent to rodent through fleas. Plague can wipe out entire colonies.

Threats to prairie dogs have caused the animals' population to fall. From 1900 to 2000, the black-tailed prairie dog population fell by 98 percent. Recovering from population loss is difficult. Prairie dogs breed only once per year. Only half of the pups make it to adulthood. Some pups die from hunger. Others are killed by predators or even adult prairie dogs.

A BALANCING ACT

Humans need land to make a living. But prairie dogs lived in grasslands before humans. **Conservation** groups hope prairie dogs and humans can both use the land. These groups work with farmers and ranchers to find solutions. For example, some groups have brought black-footed ferrets to prairie dog colonies. They hope these predators will help control the prairie dog population in a natural way.

CHAPTER 4

PROTECTING PRAIRIE DOGS

Habitat loss is a major threat to prairie dog populations. Conservation groups protect grasslands and prairie dog habitats. These groups are made up of wildlife biologists and other experts.

Conservationists work with local people to manage prairie dog colonies.

Conservationists put tags on prairie dogs to track and study the animals.

They discuss concerns with farmers and ranchers. In some cases, they relocate prairie dogs.

Relocation can be a difficult process. First, workers find a new habitat. Then they catch the prairie dogs. To do this, they fill traps with vegetables and grains. The workers then load the prairie dogs

BUBBLING BURROWS

Sometimes, workers flush prairie dogs from their burrows. They pump soapy water into the tunnels. The bubbles provide the prairie dogs with air to breathe. Then the workers wait at the entrances. They catch the prairie dogs and wipe them down. They remove soap from the animals' eyes. After that, the prairie dogs are ready to be relocated.

A conservationist cares for a prairie dog that is being relocated.

into carriers. They use hay or soft towels as cushions.

In the new habitat, the workers build a starter home. They dig out a simple burrow and place nesting boxes inside. They also build tunnels that lead to the surface. At the top of the tunnels is a mesh cage. That way, the prairie dogs can leave the burrow, but they can't run away.

Once the animals are comfortable, the workers remove the cage.

People can prevent prairie dogs from moving to certain places. Prairie dogs often cause problems in places like gardens and soccer fields. Barriers prevent prairie dogs from moving to these areas. Prairie dogs like to live in open areas. This means they will avoid places with fences or tall plants.

Conservationists also protect prairie dogs from plague. They apply a flea-killing powder to colonies. This keeps the disease from spreading.

An important part of conservation is education. Conservationists teach

A conservationist sprays a prairie dog burrow to kill fleas.

others about prairie dogs. They talk to farmers, ranchers, and even children at zoos. Many people do not understand this keystone species. They think prairie dogs only eat and dig. But these animals are important to the environment. Human understanding is key to prairie dogs' survival.

FOCUS ON
PRAIRIE DOGS

Write your answers on a separate piece of paper.

1. Write a paragraph describing how other animals rely on prairie dogs.

2. Do you think ranchers and prairie dogs can share grasslands? Why or why not?

3. How did prairie dogs get their name?
   - **A.** They are good at digging.
   - **B.** They bark to communicate.
   - **C.** They look similar to dogs.

4. How would an increase in the prairie dog population affect the black-footed ferret?
   - **A.** Black-footed ferrets would have more food to eat.
   - **B.** Prairie dogs would begin hunting black-footed ferrets.
   - **C.** The black-footed ferret population would decrease.

Answer key on page 32.

GLOSSARY

adapt
To change over time to deal with a certain situation.

colony
A group of animals that live together.

conservation
The careful protection of plants, animals, and natural resources so they are not lost or wasted.

ecosystem
The collection of living things in a natural area.

endangered
In danger of dying out.

erosion
The act of wearing away a surface.

fertilize
To make soil more fertile, or able to make plants grow.

nutrients
Substances that humans, animals, and plants need to stay healthy and strong.

predators
Animals that hunt other animals for food.

ranchers
People who own large farms for raising horses or cattle.

TO LEARN MORE

BOOKS

Bjorklund, Ruth. *24 Hours in a Grassland*. New York: Cavendish Square, 2018.

Gish, Melissa. *Prairie Dogs*. Mankato, MN: Creative Education, 2018.

Roth, Susan L., and Cindy Trumbore. *Prairie Dog Song: The Key to Saving North America's Grasslands*. New York: Lee & Low Books, 2016.

NOTE TO EDUCATORS

Visit **www.focusreaders.com** to find lesson plans, activities, links, and other resources related to this title.

INDEX

Answer Key: 1. Answers will vary; **2.** Answers will vary; **3.** B; **4.** A